Conspiracy Theory Jokes & Riddles

Government Coverups

INTRODUCTION

Welcome to the intriguing and often perplexing world of conspiracy theory jokes and riddles. In this captivating realm, enigmas and oddities, secrets and suspicions, are met with the delightful art of humor. As we embark on this journey, we invite you to put on your tinfoil hat, adjust your surveillance camera, and join us in exploring the lighter side of the shadows.

Conspiracy theories have long been the fascination of those who ponder the mysteries of our world. These theories delve into the unknown, raising questions and planting seeds of doubt in the most unexpected places. Yet, within this labyrinth of elaborate narratives and bewildering claims, lies a wellspring of comedic potential. "Conspiracy Theory Jokes and Riddles" is your ticket to uncovering that hidden humor.

We've combed through the annals of secret societies, UFO sightings, cryptic symbols, government cover-ups, and countless other intriguing phenomena to present them to you in a light-hearted and entertaining fashion. The conspiracies that often dwell in the depths of the Internet, wrapped in an aura of mystery, are now transformed into clever riddles, puns, and witty wordplay. Our goal is to reveal that laughter can be found even in the most complex and bewildering ideas.

In the pages that follow, you'll find a rich tapestry of humor, where well-crafted jokes and mind-bending riddles coexist with theories that have captured the collective imagination. Whether you're a dedicated conspiracy theorist or someone who simply enjoys a good chuckle, this book has something for you. It offers a fresh perspective on familiar narratives and introduces you to the esoteric humor hidden within the most secretive of societies.

As you delve into "Conspiracy Theory Jokes and Riddles," you'll discover that humor can be a powerful tool for dissecting the unconventional and shining a spotlight on the enigmatic. The riddles will challenge your intellect while tickling your funny bone. With each turn of the page, you'll find yourself transported to a world where laughter and curiosity go hand in hand.

So, let's leave the world of solemn speculation behind and embrace a more playful approach to conspiracy theories. Together, we'll unlock the mysteries that hide behind the laughter, the riddles that dance in the shadows, and the jokes that tantalize our sense of wonder. Get ready to embark on a journey through the enigmatic and the absurd, guided by the wisdom that sometimes the best way to deal with a mystery is to laugh in its face.

Let's begin our adventure into "Conspiracy Theory Jokes and Riddles" and explore a world where the unexplained becomes the unexpectedly hilarious.

TOPICS

EYE OF PROVIDENCE
UFO'S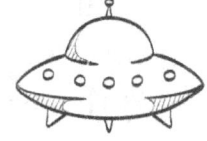
MOON LANDING

GOV'T COVERUPS

EYE OF PROVIDENCE

Q: What does AI and The Eye of Providence have in common?
A: A= 1 and I= Eye so the answer is 1 Eye.

Q: What letter does the pyramid represent?
A: The letter A

Q: Why did the Eye of Providence get a promotion?
A: Because it had an illuminating performance!

Q: What did the Eye of Providence say to the dollar bill?
A: "I've got my eye on you!"

Q: What's the Eye of Providence's favorite type of music?
A: The All-Seeing Pop!

Q: How does the Eye of Providence like its coffee?
A: With divine cream and a Freemason sugar cube!

Q: Why did the Eye of Providence join a secret society?
A: It wanted to keep an eye on things.

Q: What do you call it when the Eye of Providence throws a party?
A: An All-Seeing Soiree!

Q: What's the Eye of Providence's favorite movie?
A: "The Great Gaze-sby."

Q: How does the Eye of Providence keep its eye in good shape?
A: It does a lot of optical exercises!

Q: What did the Eye of Providence say to the triangle?
A: "I'm watching my angles."

Q: Why did the Eye of Providence become a detective?
A: To solve the mystery of the universe, one clue at a time!

Q: What's the Eye of Providence's favorite game?
A: "Hide and Illuminati Seek."

Q: What does the Eye of Providence use to take notes?
A: Its all-seeing pencil!

Q: What's the Eye of Providence's favorite social media platform?
A: Eye-book.

Q: What did the Eye of Providence say to the pyramid?
A: "You're my favorite point of view."

Q: Why was the Eye of Providence a terrible poker player?
A: Because it couldn't keep a straight eye!

Q: What's the Eye of Providence's favorite snack?
A: Illumi-nachos.

Q: Why did the Eye of Providence visit the optometrist?
A: It wanted to see if it had 20/20 divine vision.

Q: How does the Eye of Providence stay up to date with the latest news?
A: It reads the All-Seeing Times.

Q: What's the Eye of Providence's favorite kind of joke?
A: Punny ones, of course!

Q: What did the Eye of Providence say to the conspiracy theorist?
A: "I've got my eye on you, but your theories are out of sight!"

Q: How does the Eye of Providence communicate with other symbols?
A: It sends them Eye-messages.

Q: Why did the Eye of Providence refuse to watch horror movies?
A: Because it didn't want to lose its all-seeing composure.

Q: What's the Eye of Providence's favorite subject in school?
A: Geometry - it's all about the angles!

Q: How does the Eye of Providence relax?
A: It takes an Eye-laxation break

.**Q:** What did the Eye of Providence say when it won a game of cards?
A: "I see victory in my future!"

Q: Why did the Eye of Providence go to the art museum?
A: It wanted to see some "illuminating" masterpieces.

Q: What did the Eye of Providence say when it saw the compass?
A: "You're pointing in the right direction."

Q: How does the Eye of Providence take selfies?
A: It uses its divine camera.

Q: What's the Eye of Providence's favorite sport?
A: Eye-ce hockey!

Q: Why did the Eye of Providence open an optometry clinic?
A: To help others achieve their own "enlightened" vision!

Q: What did the Eye of Providence say to the telescope?
A: "You're not the only one with a long-range view."

Q: How does the Eye of Providence meditate?
A: It practices Eye-ga.

Q: What's the Eye of Providence's favorite place to vacation?
A: The Eye-rish countryside.

Q: Why did the Eye of Providence become a life coach?
A: To help people find their true calling - their "eye-deal" path!

Q: What did the Eye of Providence say to the ruler?
A: "You're good at keeping things in line."

Q: How does the Eye of Providence handle stress?
A: It practices Eye-chology.

Q: What's the Eye of Providence's favorite type of magic?
A: Optical illusions.

Q: Why did the Eye of Providence start a YouTube channel?
A: To share its "eye"-opening experiences.

Q: What did the Eye of Providence say to the lighthouse?
A: "We both shine our light on the world."

Q: How does the Eye of Providence keep its calm during turbulent times?
A: It practices Eye-ditation.

Q: What's the Eye of Providence's favorite weather?
A: High visibility.

Q: Why did the Eye of Providence become a weather forecaster?
A: It wanted to predict "clear" skies and "illuminating" days.

Q: What did the Eye of Providence say to the mirror?
A: "I see my true reflection."

Q: How does the Eye of Providence navigate through life's challenges?
A: It follows its inner compass.

Q: What's the Eye of Providence's favorite constellation?
A: The All-Seeing Eye-sis.

Q: Why did the Eye of Providence become a motivational speaker?
A: To inspire others to "see" their full potential.

Q: What did the Eye of Providence say to the traffic light?
A: "We both keep things moving smoothly."

Q: How does the Eye of Providence make decisions?
A: It uses its inner compass to point the way.

Q: What's the Eye of Providence's favorite board game?
A: "Eye-spy" the board game.

Q: Why did the Eye of Providence become a life coach for shapes?
A: It wanted to help them find their "true angles."

Q: What did the Eye of Providence say to the map?
A: "You show me the way, just like my compass."

Q: How does the Eye of Providence handle disagreements?
A: It encourages others to "see eye to eye."

Q: What's the Eye of Providence's favorite planet?
A: The one with the most visibility!

Q: Why did the Eye of Providence start a podcast?
A: To discuss "eye"-opening topics and interviews.

Q: What did the Eye of Providence say to the spotlight?
A: "We both shine a light on important matters."

Q: How does the Eye of Providence organize its thoughts?
A: It creates a "mind map."

Q: Why did the Eye of Providence get a job as a security guard?
A: Because it could keep an "eye" out for trouble!

Q: What did the Eye of Providence say to the photographer?
A: "I appreciate your ability to capture the perfect angles!"

Q: How does the Eye of Providence stay fit?
A: It practices "Eye-robics" regularly.

Q: What's the Eye of Providence's favorite type of cuisine?
A: Illumi-nese food.

Q: Why did the Eye of Providence become a tour guide?
A: To show people the sights and provide an "illuminating" experience.

Q: What did the Eye of Providence say to the mirror?
A: "You and I reflect on life's mysteries."

Q: How does the Eye of Providence handle its finances?
A: It keeps a close watch on its investments.

Q: What's the Eye of Providence's favorite dance move?
A: The "Eye"-robics shuffle.

Q: Why did the Eye of Providence start a fashion blog?
A: To share its "all-seeing" style tips.

Q: What did the Eye of Providence say to the traffic cop?
A: "We both ensure things flow smoothly."

Q: How does the Eye of Providence stay up-to-date with technology?
A: It's always on the lookout for the latest "eye"-gadgets.

Q: What's the Eye of Providence's favorite song?
A: "Eye of the Tiger" by Survivor.

Q: Why did the Eye of Providence take up gardening?
A: It wanted to grow its own "all-seeing" plants.

Q: What did the Eye of Providence say to the lighthouse?
A: "We both guide the way in our own unique style."

Q: How does the Eye of Providence handle life's puzzles?
A: It uses its "all-seeing" insight to find solutions.

Q: What's the Eye of Providence's favorite sport to watch?
A: Eye-cing.

Q: Why did the Eye of Providence become a crossword puzzle enthusiast?
A: It loved the challenge of "illuminating" words.

Q: What did the Eye of Providence say to the compass?
A: "We both point the way forward."

Q: How does the Eye of Providence relax at the beach?
A: It enjoys some "all-seeing" sunbathing.

Q: What's the Eye of Providence's favorite mode of transportation?
A: An "all-seeing" hot air balloon.

Q: Why did the Eye of Providence become an art critic?
A: It had an eye for detail.

Q: What did the Eye of Providence say to the microscope?
A: "We both help people see what's hidden."

Q: How does the Eye of Providence enjoy stargazing?
A: It loves observing the "all-seeing" constellations.

Q: What's the Eye of Providence's favorite holiday?
A: "Eye"-ster.

Q: Why did the Eye of Providence become a bird watcher?
A: Because it appreciated their "all-seeing" abilities.

Q: What did the Eye of Providence say to the telescope?
A: "We both explore the farthest reaches of the universe."

Q: How does the Eye of Providence handle its finances?
A: It invests in "illuminating" stocks.

Q: What's the Eye of Providence's favorite animal?
A: The owl, for its wise and all-seeing nature.

Q: Why did the Eye of Providence become a detective?
A: To solve mysteries and keep an "eye" on the truth.

Q: What did the Eye of Providence say to the mirror?
A: "I see my true self."

Q: How does the Eye of Providence relax by the pool?
A: It lounges and enjoys the "all-seeing" view.

Q: What's the Eye of Providence's favorite type of movie?
A: Mysteries, because it loves to watch events unfold.

Q: Why did the Eye of Providence become a gardener?
A: To cultivate an "all-seeing" garden of knowledge.

Q: What did the Eye of Providence say to the compass?
A: "We both point the way towards the truth."

Q: How does the Eye of Providence unwind after a long day?
A: It practices "Eye"-robics to relax.

Q: What's the Eye of Providence's favorite way to learn?
A: By keeping an "all-seeing" eye on books.

Q: Why did the Eye of Providence become a motivational speaker?
A: To inspire others to "see" their potential.

Q: What did the Eye of Providence say to the traffic light?
A: "My eyes see the green light, lets move."

Q: How does the Eye of Providence celebrate a successful day?
A: It throws an "All-Seeing" party!

UFO'S

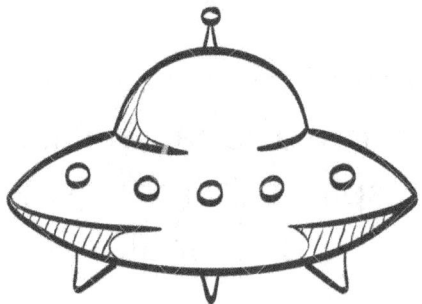

Q: Why don't aliens ever tell jokes?
A: Because they're afraid they'll abduct-lutely abduct everyone's sense of humor!

Q: How do you organize a space party?
A: You "planet" ahead!

Q: "Why did the alien refuse to play cards at the Roswell crash site?
A: Because it was afraid of getting a "bad hand"!
Q: What do you get when you cross a UFO and a dog?
A: An unidentified barking object!

Q: What do you call an alien who loves music?
A: An astro-noted musician.

Q: How do aliens keep their pants up?
A: With an "unidentified flying belt."

Q: Why don't aliens use social media?
A: Because they're afraid of the "unfriend-ly" atmosphere!

Q: How do you throw a space party?
A: You "planet" and "orbit" some good food!

Q: What did the alien say to the garden?
A: "Take me to your weeder."

Q: What's an alien's favorite candy?
A: Mars-bars.

Q: Why did the alien bring a ladder to Earth?
A: Because it wanted to take a "close encounter" selfie!

Q: What do you call an alien that tells jokes?
A: A "comedi-an."

Q: What do you call an alien spaceship that's always late?
A: An "out-of-this-world" delay.

Q: Why did the UFO apply for a job?
A: It wanted steady "flying saucers."

Q: What's an alien's favorite type of computer?
A: One with an "extraterrestrial" drive!

Q: How do aliens pay for things on Earth?
A: With "Starbucks"!

Q: Why don't aliens play hide and seek?
A: Because good luck hiding when you're "out of this world"!

Q: What do you call an alien that's a great chef?
A: A "cosmic cook."

Q: Why did the alien bring a pencil to the spaceship?
A: To draw "close encounters" with humans!

Q: What do you call an alien's favorite place to swim?
A: The "unidentified floating object."

Q: What do you call an alien that's always feeling under the weather?
A: An "unwell-ien."

Q: How do aliens stay healthy?
A: They exercise by "UFO-ing" to the gym.

Q: What do you call a polite alien?
A: A "respec-tor" of Earth's customs.

Q: What's an alien's favorite game?
A: Space invaders!

Q: How do aliens make phone calls?
A: They use their "inter-galactic" plan.

Q: Why do aliens love fast food?
A: Because it's "abduct-ively" delicious!

Q: What's an alien's favorite dance?
A: The "interstellar" shuffle!

Q: Why do aliens avoid Earth's fashion trends?
A: They don't want to look "far out" of style.

Q: What's an alien's favorite currency?
A: Flying saucer coins!

Q: Why did the alien start a band?
A: To create some "out-of-this-world" music!

Q: What do you call an alien that's always cold?
A: An "ex-icicle."

Q: Where was the biggest coverup regarding UFO's in history?
A: Roswell

Q: How many crashes were there in 1947?
A: There were actually 2 crashes

Q: What was the secret committee called that held secret meetings on UFO's?
A: MJ12 or Majestic 12

Q: What's an alien's favorite TV show?
A: "My Favorite Martian."

Q: Why did the alien apply for a job as an astronaut?
A: It wanted to see if Earth had any "out-of-this-world" job opportunities.

Q: What do you call an alien with musical talent?
A: A "space jam-mer."

Q: How do aliens communicate with each other?
A: They use "extraterrestrial" messaging services.

Q: What's an alien's favorite subject in school?
A: "Astro-nomy."

Q: What do you call an alien that tells funny stories?
A: A "comic-ET."

Q: Why don't aliens play cards on Earth?
A: Because they're afraid of getting a "bad hand."

Q: How do aliens stay cool in the summer?
A: They visit the "abduct-ual" swimming pools.

Q: Why did the alien invite humans to a dance party on their spaceship?
A: They wanted to teach us the "space-walk"!

Q: What's an alien's favorite instrument?
A: The "cosmo-flute."

Q: How do aliens celebrate birthdays?
A: With a "cosmic cake" and "interstellar" gifts!

Q: What do you call an alien that loves gardening?
A: An "astro-botanist."

Q: Why did the UFO enroll in a dance class?
A: It wanted to master the "flying saucer shuffle."

Q: How do aliens greet each other?
A: They say, "Take me to your leader."

Q: What's an alien's favorite drink?
A: "Space-uccino."

Q: Why did the alien get a job as a lifeguard?
A: They wanted to ensure that beachgoers were safe from "alien-tidal waves."

Q: How do aliens have fun at amusement parks?
A: They ride the "roller-asteroid."

Q: What do you call an alien's favorite vehicle?
A: A "spaceship.

Q: Why do aliens make terrible comedians?
A: Because their jokes are always "out of this world"!

Q: How do aliens keep their spaceships clean?
A: With "unidentified flying mops."

Q: Why did the alien apply for a job as a tour guide on Earth?
A: They wanted to show visitors the "extraterrestrial" sights.

Q: How do aliens navigate through space traffic?
A: They use their "galactic GPS."

Q: Why did the alien bring a dictionary to the spaceship?
A: To understand Earth's "alien" language.

Q: What's an alien's favorite exercise?
A: The "cosmic cardio."

Q: How do aliens stay hydrated in space?
A: With "UFO-nade."

Q: Why do aliens love to visit the beach?
A: Because they enjoy "unidentified floating objects."

Q: What's an alien's favorite fruit?
A: "Starfruit."

Q: Why did the alien become a chef?
A: They wanted to create "interstellar" cuisine.

Q: How do aliens play board games?
A: They use "UFO-fficial" game pieces.

Q: Why do UFOs always use turn signals?
A: Because even aliens know the importance of "signaling" their intentions!

Q: Why do UFOs make terrible comedians?
A: Because their humor is always "flying over" our heads!

Q: What's a UFO's favorite mode of communication?
A: Crop circles - it's their way of leaving a "message in the field"!

Q: How do UFOs keep their passengers entertained during long trips?
A: They have "stellar" in-flight movies, of course!

Q: Why did the UFO start a fashion blog?
A: Because they wanted to share their "out-of-this-world" style tips!

Q: What's an alien's favorite card game on a UFO?
A: Solitaire - they love playing cards alone while they're on a "solo-air" mission!

Q: Why do UFOs love to visit Earth's fast-food restaurants?
A: Because they're fascinated by the concept of "drive-thru" abduction!

Q: What's an alien's favorite kind of transportation?
A: UFOber - they love getting around using unidentified flying Ubers!

Q: Why did the UFO apply for a job as a DJ?
A: Because it wanted to make the entire galaxy dance to its "out-of-this-world" beats!

Q: What do UFOs do before taking off?
A: They make sure to check their "flight-planets."

Q: Why did the UFO break up with its spaceship?
A: It wanted some space!

Q: What's a UFO's favorite exercise?
A: Flying saucerobics!

Q: Why did the UFO go to therapy?
A: It had too many abduction issues!

Q: What's a UFO's favorite party game?
A: Cosmic Twister!

Q: Why did the alien sit next to the computer?
A: It wanted to keep an eye on the mouse!

Q: How do UFOs send secret messages?
A: They use "extraterrestrial" mail!

Q: What's a UFO's favorite type of humor?
A: "Galactic" jokes that are truly universal!

Q: Why did the UFO start a vegetable garden?
A: It wanted to grow its own "unidentified flying objects"!

Q: What do you call an alien that can sing?
A: An astro-notable!

Q: Why do UFOs never play hide and seek?
A: Because they're always spotted!

Q: What's a alien's favorite kind of chocolate?
A: Mars-bars!

Q: Why did the alien become a stand-up comedian?
A: It wanted to bring some "cosmic" humor to Earth!

Q: What's an alien's favorite social media platform?
A: Space-book!

Q: Why did the UFO start a workout routine?
A: It wanted to get into "flying saucer" shape!

Q: What's an alien's favorite TV show?
A: The X-Files

Q: What's a alien's favorite genre of music?
A: Celestial!

Q: Why did the alien join a band?
A: It wanted to be the lead "guitar-ship" player!

Q: What's an alien's favorite cereal?
A: "Starry Flakes" the breakfast of extraterrestrial champions!

Q: Why did the alien enroll in a cooking class?
A: It wanted to master the art of "intergalactic cuisine."

Q: What do you call an alien with a great sense of humor?
A: A "comet-ian."

Q: Why did the alien start a podcast?
A: It had out-of-this-world stories to share!

Q: Why did the alien become a gardener?
A: It wanted to learn how to "crop circle" properly!

Q: What's a alien's favorite school subject?
A: Astro-nomy!

Q: Why did the alien become a motivational speaker?
A: To inspire others to reach for the stars!

Q: What do alien's say when they land on Earth?
A: "Take me to your litter box!"

Q: Why did the alien go to therapy?
A: It had a close encounter with its feelings!

Q: What's an alien's favorite social media platform?
A: Instagram, for its out-of-this-world filters!

Q: Why do UFOs never play hide and seek?
A: Because they always stand out!

Q: What do you call a alien with a great memory?
A: An "extraterrestrial eidetic."

Q: What's an alien's favorite type of comedy?
A: Stand-up cosmology!

Q: Why did an aliens become a detective?
A: It wanted to solve the mysteries of the universe!

Q: What do UFOs do for fun on Earth?
A: They go "crop circling" in the fields!

Q: Why did the alien go to the party?
A: It wanted to "abduct" attention!

Q: What's an alien's favorite board game?
A: Settlers of Saturn!

Q: Why did the UFO apply for a job as a teacher?
A: It wanted to give lessons on "interplanetary relations."

Q: What do you call a aliens that's really good at math?
A: A "calcu-lunar."

Q: Why did the alien get kicked out of the library?
A: It refused to "be quiet" and kept humming space tunes!

Q: What's an alien's favorite snack?
A: "Cosmic popcorn" — it's truly otherworldly!

Q: Why did the alien go to therapy?
A: It was feeling a bit spaced out!

Q: What's a UFO's favorite type of pasta?
A: "Spaghe-tie-in."

Q: Why did the aliens start a band?
A: It wanted to play "fly-fi" music!

Q: What do you call a UFO with a great sense of direction?
A: An "astro-navigator."

Q: Why did the alien become a tour guide?
A: It knew all the "alien hotspots"!

Q: What's an alien's favorite type of joke?
A: One that's "out of this world" funny!

Q: What do aliens say when they break up with their Earth lovers?
A: It's not you, it's Uranus!"

Q: Why did the UFO start a gardening club?
A: It wanted to see if Earth's plants were as "alien" as its own.

Q: How do aliens apologize?
A: They send "extraterrestrial" cards.

Q: Why did the UFO go to therapy?
A: It had too many "unresolved flying saucer" issues.

Q: What's a aliens favorite type of movie?
A: "Close Encounters of the Third Kindergarten."

Q: Why did the alien refuse to play hide and seek?
A: It didn't want to be labeled as a "hide-behind-the-bush" enthusiast.

Q: What do you call a UFO in disguise?
A: An "unidentified fashion object."

Q: Why did the alien become a stand-up philosopher?
A: It had a knack for delivering "stellar" advice.

Q: How do aliens write love letters?
A: With plenty of "space-y" puns.

Q: Why did the alien apply for a job at the bakery?
A: It heard they were looking for someone with a "stellar" pastry chef.

Q: What do aliens use to clean their windows?
A: "Astro-Windex."

Q: What's an alien's favorite social media platform?
A: "Spacebook" – where they post updates about their cosmic adventures.

Q: Why did the alien with a UFO apply for a job at the circus?
A: It had a talent for "flying saucer balancing."

Q: What do you call a alien that loves to sing?
A: An "astro-melodist."

Q: Why did the alien with a spaceship start a workout routine?
A: It wanted to be the "fittest" ship in the galaxy.

Q: What's an alien's favorite Earth holiday?
A: "Halloween" – they love blending in with the costumes.

Q: Why did the alien refuse to play poker?
A: It didn't want to deal with "alien" hands.

Q: What's a aliens favorite type of sandwich?
A: "cosmic wrap."

Q: Why did the alien become a chef?
A: It heard Earth had the best "unidentified frying objects."

Q: What's an alien's favorite Earth TV show?
A: "Cooking with the Humans."

Q: Why did the UFO bring a map to Earth?
A: It wanted to make sure it didn't accidentally land in the Bermuda Triangle.

Q: What do UFOs do on vacation?
A: They visit "unidentified relaxation spots."

Q: Why did the UFO join a band?
A: It wanted to play "intergalactic rock."

Q: What's a aliens favorite type of joke?
A: One that's out of orbit

Q: Why did the alien become a motivational speaker?
A: It wanted to spread the message of "interstellar inspiration."

MOON LANDING

Q: Why did the moon start a comedy club?
A: Because it had a great sense of "lunar-tics."

Q: What do you call a moon that can sing?
A: A lunar crooner.

Q: Why did the moon refuse to play hide and seek?
A: It said it always felt "exposed."

Q: How does the moon clean its house?
A: With a comet.

Q: Why did the moon get a job at the bakery?
A: It loved making "half-moons."

Q: What did the astronaut say to the moon?
A: "You're a space-ial friend."

Q: How does the moon cut its sandwiches?
A: Into moon-iches.

Q: Why did the moon break up with the sun?
A: It needed some "space."

Q: Why did the moon start a rock band?
A: Because it had an "out-of-this-world" sound.

Q: How does the moon stay cool during summer?
A: It has a "lunar fan."

Q: Why did the moon apply for a job at the art gallery?
A: It wanted to showcase its "full artistry."

Q: What's the moon's favorite dance move?
A: The crescent shuffle.

Q: Why did the moon go to therapy?
A: It had too many phases to work through.

Q: What's the moon's favorite game?
A: Hide and crater-seek.

Q: Why did the moon bring a ladder to the party?
A: It wanted to reach the "full potential."

Q: How does the moon cut a pizza?
A: Into "lunar slices."

Q: What did the astronaut say to the moon when he forgot his keys?
A: "Can I get a lift?"

Q: Why did the moon become a stand-up comedian?
A: Because it had great "lunar-tic timing."

Q: What's the moon's favorite type of humor?
A: Punny-phases.

Q: Why did the moon apply for a job at the bakery?
A: It heard they were looking for someone with a "stellar" pastry chef.

Q: How does the moon communicate with other celestial bodies?
A: It "radiates" good vibes.

Q: Why did the moon get a speeding ticket?
A: It was caught in a full mooning.

Q: What do you call a moon that's always singing?
A: A lunar-tune.

Q: Why did the moon bring a pencil to the party?
A: In case it wanted to draw attention to itself.

Q: How does the moon throw a party?
A: It has a "celestial ball."

Q: Why did the moon start a fitness blog?
A: It wanted to share its "lunar fitness" routine.

Q: What's the moon's favorite cereal?
A: Cheerios – it likes things that go round.

Q: Why did the moon become a detective?
A: It wanted to solve the mystery of the missing stars.

Q: What's the moon's favorite school subject?
A: Space-ematics.

Q: Why did the moon break up with its girlfriend?
A: She was always trying to "eclipse" its brilliance.

Q: What do you call a moon with a big ego?
A: An "astronomical narcissist."

Q: How does the moon get a tan?
A: It waits for a solar flare.

Q: What do you call a moon that's always telling jokes?
A: A lunar joker.

Q: Why did the moon go to the spa?
A: It needed some "lunar relaxation."

Q: What's the moon's favorite sport?
A: Lunar-golf.

Q: Why did the moon start a podcast?
A: It had a lot of "spacey" thoughts to share.

Q: How does the moon fix its computer?
A: It presses "lunar" restart.

Q: Why did the moon become a baker?
A: It loved kneading "moon dough."

Q: What do you call a moon that's always moving?
A: "mover and shaker."

Q: Why did the astronaut bring a sandwich to the moon?
A: In case he got "hungry for space."

Q: What's the moon's favorite movie genre?
A: Space-terpieces.

Q: Why did the moon go to therapy?
A: It needed someone to talk to about its "crater" issues.

Q: Why did the moon become a librarian?
A: It wanted to "shine a light" on great literature.

Q: What's the moon's favorite type of tea?
A: Celestial-lestial.

Q: Why did the moon bring a camera to the party?
A: It wanted to capture the "lunar memories."

Q: How does the moon end a relationship?
A: It says, "It's time for a 'crescent uncoupling.'"

Q: Why did the moon become a poet?
A: It had a way with "lunar-tic verses."

Q: What's the moon's favorite mode of transportation?
A: A "crescent car."

Q: Why did the moon become a chef?
A: It loved creating dishes that were truly "out of this world."

Q: What do you call a moon that's always singing opera?
A: A "lunar-diva."

Q: Why did the moon go to the concert?
A: It heard the band was playing "interstellar tunes."

Q: How does the moon read a map?
A: It follows the "star charts."

Q: Why did the moon become an artist?
A: It loved painting "stellar masterpieces."

Q: What do you call a moon that's always laughing?
A: A "lunar-tic giggle."

Q: Why did the moon go to the spa?
A: It needed a little "lunar pampering."

Q: What's the moon's favorite game?
A: "Orbit and Seek."

Q: Why did the astronaut bring a ladder to the moon?
A: Because he wanted to take "one small step for man" and "one giant leap for mankind."

Moon Landing Phrase
"One Small Step for Man" and "One Giant Leap for Mankind."

Q: Why did the astronaut bring a ladder to the moon?
A: Because he wanted to take "one small step for man" and "one giant leap for mankind."

Q: How does an astronaut apologize?
A: "I'm sorry if I took one small step on your foot, but it's a giant leap for my dance moves."

Q: Why did the moon refuse to dance?
A: It said, "I can't follow those 'one small step for man' instructions!"

Q: What did the moon say to the sun at the cosmic party?
A: "Your rays are great, but my steps are one small and my leaps are giant!"

Q: Why did the astronaut become a chef?
A: He wanted to create dishes that were "one small bite for man" but a "giant feast for mankind."

Q: How do astronauts order coffee?
A: "I'll have one small espresso for man and a giant latte for mankind."

Q: Why did the astronaut bring a pen to the moon?
A: He wanted to take "one small doodle for man" and create a "giant masterpiece for mankind."

Q: What did the astronaut say to his friend at the gym?
A: "I just took one small lift for man, but it felt like a giant bench press for mankind."

Q: Why did the astronaut break up with his girlfriend?
A: He said, "Our relationship was one small commitment for man but a giant leap for my personal space."

Q: How does an astronaut order pizza?
A: "I'll take one small pepperoni for man and a giant supreme for mankind."

Q: Why did the moon start a fitness blog?
A: It wanted to inspire everyone to take "one small jog for man" and a "giant marathon for mankind."

Q: What did the astronaut say to his dentist?
A: "I just had one small filling for man, but it felt like a giant root canal for mankind."

Q: Why did the astronaut apply for a job as a comedian?
A: He wanted to deliver jokes that were "one small chuckle for man" but a "giant laugh for mankind."

Q: How does an astronaut apologize for a mistake?
A: "I'm sorry if that was one small error for man, but it turned out to be a giant blunder for mankind."

Q: Why did the moon start a band?
A: It wanted to play music that was "one small note for man" but a "giant symphony for mankind."

Q: What did the astronaut say to his friend who forgot his keys?
A: "Looks like you'll be taking one small bus for man and a giant taxi for mankind."

Q: Why did the astronaut bring a map to the moon?
A: He wanted to take "one small route for man" but a "giant expedition for mankind."

Q: How does an astronaut apologize for stepping on someone's toes?
A: "I'm sorry if that was one small stomp for man, but it felt like a giant leap on your foot for mankind."

Q: Why did the moon start a dance studio?
A: It wanted to teach everyone to take "one small cha-cha for man" and a "giant tango for mankind."

Q: What did the astronaut say to his friend with a small car?
A: "You may have one small hatchback for man, but it's a giant SUV for mankind."

GOV'T COVERUPS

Q: Why did the government official bring a ladder to the conspiracy meeting?
A: They wanted to ensure they were always one step ahead of the truth.

Q: How does the government keep a secret?
A: They make it a "classified" joke.

Q: Why did the conspiracy theorist apply for a job in government?
A: To finally get to the bottom of the coverup... or so they think.

Q: What's the government's favorite board game?
A: Coverup-oly.

Q: Why did the conspiracy theorist start a bakery?
A: They heard the government was hiding the best dough.

Q: What do you call a government coverup in the winter?
A: A snow-conspiracy.

Q: Why did the alien refuse to testify about the government coverup?
A: It didn't want to get "probed" for information.

Q: How does the government organize a secret party?
A: They send out "classified" invitations.

Q: Why did the conspiracy theorist go to therapy?
A: They needed someone to validate their beliefs.

Q: What's the government's favorite type of pizza?
A: "Cover-up-pepperoni."

Q: Why did the government agent become a gardener?
A: To learn the art of planting "classified seeds."

Q: How do government officials stay fit?
A: They do "cover-up calisthenics."

Q: Why did the conspiracy theorist cross the road?
A: To avoid the government's surveillance cameras on the other side.

Q: What's the government's favorite song?
A: "Can't Stop the Coverup" by The Classified Files.

Q: Why did the conspiracy theorist start a podcast?
A: They wanted to spread the "unfiltered truth."

Q: What do you call a government coverup in a library?
A: "hush-hush" conspiracy.

Q: Why did the government coverup attend therapy?
A: It needed someone to help "unmask" its true feelings.

Q: How does the government hide its snacks?
A: In "covert containers."

Q: Why did the conspiracy theorist get a job at the zoo?
A: They heard the government was hiding the truth about talking animals.

Q: What's the government's favorite dance move?
A: The "classified shuffle."

Q: Why did the conspiracy theorist start a fashion line?
A: They wanted to reveal the "hidden patterns" in clothing.

Q: What's the government's favorite board game?
A: Monopoly, because they love controlling the narrative.

Q: Why did the conspiracy theorist bring a map to the government building?
A: To find the "hidden agendas."

Q: How does the government keep secrets from leaking?
A: By sealing them with a "classified" kiss.

Q: Why did the conspiracy theorist join a band?
A: They wanted to play the "cover-up tune."

Q: What's the government's favorite ice cream flavor?
A: "Conspiracy Chocolate Chip."

Q: Why did the government official go to therapy?
A: They needed someone to help them "redact" their emotions.

Q: How does the government make decisions?
A: By playing "classified" rock-paper-scissors.

Q: Why did the conspiracy theorist apply for a job at the bakery?
A: They heard the government was hiding the best "dough-cuments."

Q: What's the government's favorite sport?
A: "Cover-up and Seek."

Q: Why did the conspiracy theorist start a comedy club?
A: To reveal the "hidden punchlines" of the government.

Q: What do you call a government coverup at a comedy show?
A: A "classified laugh."

Q: Why did the government official become a gardener?
A: They wanted to master the art of planting "classified seeds."

Q: How does the government hide in plain sight?
A: By wearing "camou-flage."

Q: Why did the conspiracy theorist become a magician?
A: They wanted to reveal the "hidden tricks" of the government.

Q: What's the government's favorite type of car?
A: A "cover-up convertible."

Q: Why did the conspiracy theorist bring a dictionary to the government meeting?
A: To look up the meaning of "hidden agendas."

Q: What's the government's favorite type of cookie?
A: Conspiracy Snickerdoodle."

Q: Why did the government official start a podcast?
A: To share the "classified stories" of their adventures.

Q: How does the government relax?
A: With a game of "cover-up and chill."

Q: Why did the conspiracy theorist start a fashion blog?
A: To expose the "hidden trends" in government attire.

Q: What's the government's favorite type of sandwich?
A: The "covert club."

Q: Why did the conspiracy theorist bring a camera to the government building?
A: To capture the "hidden evidence."

Q: What's the government's favorite holiday?
A: "Cover-up Thanksgiving."

Q: Why did the conspiracy theorist become a chef?
A: They wanted to cook up the "hidden recipes" of the government.

Q: How does the government organize a party?
A: With a "classified" guest list.

Q: Why did the government official go to the beach?
A: To bury their "classified" secrets in the sand.

Q: What's the government's favorite movie genre?
A: "Conspiracy Theor-dramas."

Q: Why did the conspiracy theorist become a detective?
A: To uncover the "hidden truths" in every case.

Q: How does the government keep a secret meeting quiet?
A: With "classified whispers."

Q: Why did the conspiracy theorist bring a flashlight to the government building?
A: To shed light on the "hidden corners."

Q: What's the government's favorite type of music?
A: "Conspiracy Rock."

Q: Why did the government official go to the comedy club?
A: To enjoy a night of "classified laughter."

Q: How does the government official play hide and seek?
A: They disappear using "classified camouflage.

Q: Why did the conspiracy theorist become a lifeguard?
A: To keep an eye on the "hidden waves" of the government.

Q: What's the government's favorite animal?
A: The "cover-up-chameleon."

Q: Why did the government official bring a calculator to the meeting?
A: To calculate the "classified math" of their decisions.

Q: How does the government keep its documents safe?
A: With a "classified lock."

Q: Why did the conspiracy theorist bring a telescope to the government building?
A: To reveal the "hidden constellations" of power.

Q: What's the government's favorite dessert?
A: "Cover-up cake."

Q: Why did the government official become a gardener?
A: To plant "classified flowers" in the garden of secrecy.

Q: How does the government hide a treasure?
A: With a "classified map."

Q: Why did the conspiracy theorist become a teacher?
A: To educate students on the "hidden curriculum."

Q: What's the government's favorite kind of sandwich?
A: A "classified club" with extra secrecy.

Q: How does the government order coffee?
A: "I'll take one small bean for man and a giant latte for mankind."

Q: Why did the conspiracy theorist start a cooking show?
A: To expose the "hidden ingredients" in government recipes.

Q: What's the government's favorite weather?
A: "Cloudy with a chance of classified information."

Q: How does the government navigate?
A: With a "classified GPS" that always takes them off the grid.

Q: Why did the conspiracy theorist start a book club?
A: To read between the lines of "classified government literature."

Q: What do you call a government official who loves to garden?
A: "classified horticulturist."

Q: Why did the government agent go to therapy?
A: Too many secrets were weighing on their "classified conscience."

Q: How does the government like its eggs?
A: "Classified" and scrambled.

Q: Why did the conspiracy theorist become a magician?
A: To make government secrets disappear in a puff of smoke.

Q: What's the government's favorite game?
A: "Monopoly," because they know how to control the conspiracy.

Q: Why did the alien refuse to attend the government party?
A: It didn't want to get "probed" for classified information.

Q: How does the government stay hydrated?
A: With a glass of "classified water.

Q: Why did the conspiracy theorist start a bakery?
A: To uncover the "secret ingredients" in government pastries.

Q: What's the government's favorite type of bread?
A: "Conspiracy sourdough" — it rises to the occasion.

Q: Why did the government official bring a map to the comedy club?
A: To find the "hidden punchlines."

Q: How does the government make decisions?
A: By playing "classified rock, paper, scissors."

Q: Why did the conspiracy theorist bring a telescope to the government building?
A: To uncover the "hidden constellations" of power.

Q: What's the government's favorite form of communication?
A: "Classified messages in a bottle."

Q: Why did the government agent apply for a job at the zoo?
A: They heard there were "classified species" to observe.

Q: How does the government send secret messages?
A: By using "classified emojis."

Q: Why did the conspiracy theorist bring a flashlight to the government meeting?
A: To shine a light on the "hidden corners" of bureaucracy.

Q: What's the government's favorite type of pasta?
A: "Conspiracy linguini" — it's full of twists and turns

Q: Why did the government official become a lifeguard?
A: To keep an eye on the "classified waves" of information.

Q: How does the government stay fit?
A: With a workout routine of "classified calisthenics."

Q: Why did the conspiracy theorist bring a camera to the government building?
A: To capture the "hidden evidence."

Q: What's the government's favorite party game?
A: "Classified charades" — guessing the secret agenda

Q: How does the government make sandwiches?
A: By spreading a layer of "classified mayo."

Q: Why did the conspiracy theorist become a detective?
A: To uncover the "hidden truths" in every case.

Q: What's the government's favorite type of chocolate?
A: "Conspiracy truffles" — with a surprise center.

Q: Why did the government official become a librarian?
A: To "classify" great literature.

Q: How does the government relax?
A: With a game of "classified chess."

Q: How does the government handle stress?
A: With a cup of "classified herbal tea."

Q: Why did the conspiracy theorist start a fashion blog?
A: To expose the "hidden trends" in government attire.

Q: What's the government's favorite mode of transportation?
A: A "classified car" with tinted windows.

Q: Why did the government agent bring a ladder to the bar?
A: To always stay one step ahead of the conspiracy.

Q: Why did the conspiracy theorist bring a magnifying glass to the government meeting?
A: To zoom in on the "hidden agendas."

Q: What's the government's favorite type of fruit?
A: "Classified bananas" — top secret nutrition.

Q: Why did the government official become a tour guide?
A: To navigate through the "classified hotspots."

Q: How does the government decorate for holidays?
A: With "classified ornaments" on the tree.

Q: Why did the conspiracy theorist bring a dictionary to the government meeting?
A: To look up the meaning of "hidden agendas."

Q: What's the government's favorite candy?
A: "Conspiracy gummies" — full of secret flavors.

Q: Why did the government official go to therapy?
A: To work through the "classified stress."

Q: How does the government organize a secret party?
A: With a "classified" guest list.

Q: Why did the conspiracy theorist bring a telescope to the comedy club?
A: To see the "hidden punchlines."

Q: What's the government's favorite type of cake?
A: "Cover-up cheesecake" — with layers of secrecy.

Q: Why did the government agent apply for a job at the bakery?
A: To ensure the "classified dough" was well-protected.

SECRET WORDS THAT HAVE AI IN IT

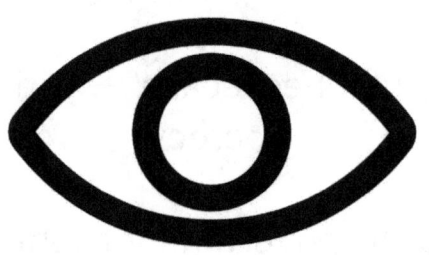

C I A: IA
Q: Guess what the "C" stands for?
A: Central

Q: Now in reverse order what does "AIC" stand for?
A: 1 eye centrally watching you.

Q: What is the bird on the CIA's symbol represent?
A: The eagle

Q: What are eagles known for?
A: Their eyes, which has good vision

Q: What letter does the 9 represent in the alphabet?
A: "I"

Q: What does A9 camera mean?
A: 1 eye camera

Q: AI Stands for what technology?
A: Artificial Intelligence.

Q: On the CBS tv Network Logo what number of the alphabet is the letter "S"?
A: 19, Meaning 1=A and 9=I

Q: What symbol does the CBS logo have?
A: 1 Eye

Q: The bitten apple on the Apple logo symbolizes what?
A: Knowledge, from the Garden of Eden.

Q: When you make your password visible online, what's watching you?
A: 1 eye

Q: When someone's eyes are opened it symbolizes what?
A: Knowledge

Q: What is the hidden meaning in reverse for the emergency number 911 REMOVING THE LAST 1?
A: 1=1 and 9=I so it's 1 Eye

Q: When you pronounce the word Evil backwards you get what?
A: Live

FUNNY FACTS

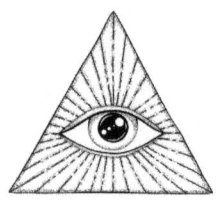

The Eye of Providence

Why the Eye of Providence joined a secret society?

The Eye of Providence, with its all-seeing gaze, made a conscious decision to join a secret society for one primary reason - it wanted to keep an eye on everything. As an ancient symbol representing divine providence and omniscience, the Eye understood the power and knowledge that could be gained by being part of a clandestine organization. By becoming a member of this secretive group, the Eye believed it would have
.

access to information and insights that would otherwise remain hidden from ordinary individuals.

Joining a secret society provided the Eye with an opportunity to delve into the depths of human nature and explore the intricate web of connections that shape our world. It sought to uncover hidden truths, unravel mysteries, and gain a deeper understanding of the forces at play behind closed doors. The Eye recognized that within these societies lay ancient wisdom, esoteric knowledge, and powerful networks that could potentially influence the course of history.

Moreover, by aligning
itself with like-minded individuals who shared
its insatiable curiosity and thirst for
knowledge, the Eye found solace in knowing
that it was not alone in its pursuit. It craved
intellectual stimulation and sought
companionship among those who were equally
committed to unraveling life's enigmas. In
joining a secret society, the Eye hoped to find
kindred spirits who would challenge
its perceptions, broaden its horizons, and
push it further along its path of enlightenment

The Eye of Providence as a detective

With its innate ability to observe every detail without bias or prejudice, it was only natural for the Eye of Providence to become a detective. Always watching for clues, this all-seeing symbol possessed an uncanny knack for piecing together disparate fragments into coherent narratives. Its keen perception allowed it to see beyond what met the eye and discern patterns where others saw chaos.

The Eye of Providence as a security guard

The decision for the Eye of Providence to become a security guard was driven by its innate desire to protect and safeguard. With its watchful gaze and unwavering vigilance, this symbol understood the importance of maintaining order and ensuring the safety of individuals and their surroundings.

As a security guard, the Eye took on the responsibility of monitoring and assessing potential threats with unparalleled precision. Its ability to see beyond what lay on the surface allowed it to identify suspicious activities or individuals that might otherwise go unnoticed. The Eye's presence alone served as a deterrent, reminding would-be wrongdoers that they were being watched.

In addition to its role in preventing crime, the Eye of Providence also played a crucial part in crisis management. Its ability to remain calm under pressure and make quick decisions based on real-time observations proved invaluable in emergency situations. Whether it was responding to natural disasters or handling security breaches, the Eye's unwavering focus ensured that chaos could be contained and lives protected.

Furthermore, as a security guard, the Eye became an integral part of creating safe spaces for individuals to thrive. By diligently monitoring access points and enforcing protocols, it contributed to fostering an environment where people could feel secure and focus on their endeavors without fear or distraction.

UFOs

Why aliens don't eat clowns?

When it comes to the question of why aliens don't eat clowns, there are several theories that can shed light on this peculiar phenomenon. One possible explanation is that clowns, with their exaggerated makeup and colorful costumes, may appear strange and unsettling to extraterrestrial beings. Aliens might not be familiar with the concept of clowns as entertainers and could perceive them as a potential threat or source of confusion.

Another theory suggests that aliens have different dietary preferences than humans. It is possible that their physiology and digestive systems are not compatible with the nutritional requirements of clown meat. Just like how some animals have specific diets based on their biological needs, aliens might have evolved to consume certain types of food that do not include clowns.

Furthermore, it is worth considering the possibility that aliens simply do not find clowns appetizing. Taste preferences can vary greatly between species, and what humans find delicious might not appeal to extraterrestrial palates. Clowns are known for their comedic performances rather than being culinary delicacies, so it is plausible that aliens have no interest in consuming them.

Additionally, there could be cultural or ethical reasons behind why aliens refrain from eating clowns. Just as humans have cultural taboos surrounding certain foods, such as dogs or insects in some societies, aliens may have their own set of norms and values regarding what is acceptable to eat. Clowns might hold a special status in alien culture or folklore, making them off-limits for consumption.

Aliens With Three Eyes

The concept of aliens with three eyes has long been a staple in science fiction and popular culture. While it may seem fantastical, there are scientific principles that can help us explore the possibility of extraterrestrial beings possessing an additional eye.

One theory suggests that aliens with three eyes could have evolved in environments where visual perception plays a crucial role. On Earth, many animals have developed multiple eyes to enhance their ability to detect predators or prey, navigate complex terrains, or perceive different wavelengths of light. It is conceivable that aliens living in environments with unique visual challenges might have evolved an extra eye to gain a competitive advantage.

Another possibility is that the third eye serves a specialized function beyond conventional vision. In some species on Earth, such as certain reptiles and birds, a third eye called the parietal eye exists but is not used for regular vision. Instead, it helps regulate circadian rhythms or detect changes in light intensity. Aliens with three eyes might possess similar adaptations that allow them to perceive aspects of their environment that are invisible to humans.

Furthermore, the concept of an additional eye could be symbolic rather than literal. In many cultures on Earth, the idea of a "third eye" represents heightened intuition or spiritual insight. If we encounter aliens who claim to possess a third eye, it could be metaphorical, indicating their advanced cognitive abilities or heightened awareness of the universe.

How Aliens Throw a Party

The idea of aliens throwing a party might conjure images of intergalactic celebrations filled with exotic foods, dazzling lights, and otherworldly entertainment. While we can only speculate about the specifics, exploring the concept of how aliens might throw a party can provide nsights into their social dynamics and cultural practices.

One possibility is that alien parties revolve around communal experiences and shared rituals. Just as humans gather to celebrate special occasions or bond with friends and family, aliens may have their own traditions that bring individuals together.

These gatherings could involve music, dance, storytelling, or other forms of artistic expression that foster a sense of unity and connection among attendees.

Another aspect to consider is the role of technology in alien parties. Given the potential advancements in extraterrestrial civilizations, it is conceivable that their parties would incorporate cutting-edge technologies for entertainment purposes. Virtual reality simulations, holographic displays, or mind-linking devices could
create immersive experiences that surpass anything currently available on Earth.

Furthermore, alien parties might feature cuisine and beverages that are completely foreign to us. Just as different cultures on Earth have distinct culinary traditions, extraterrestrial civilizations could have their own unique flavors and cooking techniques. Aliens might introduce humans to exotic dishes made from ingredients we have never encountered before or offer beverages with mind-altering properties.

Additionally, communication at alien parties could be vastly different from our human interactions. If aliens possess telepathic abilities or use non-verbal forms of communication, their parties might involve a level of interconnectedness and understanding beyond our current capabilities.

This could lead to heightened emotional connections between attendees and a deeper sense of collective consciousness.

Moon Landing

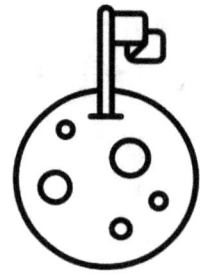

Restaurant on the Moon

The idea of a restaurant on the moon may seem like something out of science fiction, but with advancements in space exploration and technology, it could become a reality in the not-so-distant future. Imagine dining under the stars, or rather, under the Earth's view from space, while enjoying a gourmet meal prepared by top chefs. This concept opens up a whole new realm of possibilities for culinary experiences.

One of the main challenges in establishing a restaurant on the moon is creating an environment that can sustain human life.

The lack of atmosphere and extreme temperatures make it difficult for humans to survive without proper protection. However, with advancements in space architecture and engineering, scientists are exploring ways to create habitable spaces on celestial bodies like the moon.

In terms of food production, growing crops on the moon would be a significant challenge due to its harsh conditions. However, scientists have been experimenting with hydroponics and aeroponics systems that could potentially allow for sustainable food production in space. These systems involve growing plants without soil by providing them with nutrients through water or mist. By utilizing these innovative techniques, it may be possible to grow fresh produce for consumption at a lunar restaurant.

Furthermore, transporting ingredients from Earth to the moon would be costly and impractical. To overcome this challenge, scientists are researching ways to cultivate food directly on-site using local resources such as lunar regolith (moon soil) and water ice found in permanently shadowed craters. By utilizing these resources, astronauts could potentially harvest and process their own ingredients for meals at the restaurant.

Another aspect to consider is how diners would experience gravity while dining on the moon. Since there is only one-sixth of Earth's gravity on the lunar surface, traditional seating arrangements might not work as expected. Designing specialized chairs or tables that provide stability and comfort in low-gravity environments would be crucial for a successful dining experience.

Additionally, the restaurant on the moon could offer unique views and experiences that are impossible to replicate on Earth. Imagine looking out of the restaurant's windows and seeing Earth rise above the lunar horizon, or witnessing a breathtaking lunar eclipse while enjoying a meal. These awe-inspiring moments would undoubtedly create unforgettable memories for diners.

While the concept of a restaurant on the moon is still in its infancy, it represents an exciting frontier for both space exploration and gastronomy. As technology continues to advance, we may one day see astronauts and tourists alike enjoying fine dining experiences in the vastness of space.

Astronauts Catching Up on TV Shows on the Moon

When we think about astronauts living and working on the moon, catching up on TV shows might not be the first thing that comes to mind. However, just like
people on Earth, astronauts need leisure activities to relax and unwind during their downtime in space.

One might wonder how astronauts can watch TV shows while on the moon since traditional broadcasting methods are not feasible in such an environment. The answer lies in satellite technology and digital media storage systems specially designed for space missions.

NASA has developed advanced satellite dish systems that allow astronauts to receive television signals directly from Earth while stationed on the moon or aboard spacecraft orbiting it. These satellite dishes are equipped with highly sensitive receivers capable of capturing even weak signals from Earth. The signals are then transmitted to the astronauts' living quarters, where they can be viewed on specially designed screens.

To ensure that astronauts have access to a wide range of TV shows and movies, NASA has developed an extensive digital media library. This library contains a vast collection of entertainment content, including popular TV series, movies, documentaries, and educational programs. Astronauts can choose from a variety of genres and watch their favorite shows during their leisure time.

The digital media storage systems used by astronauts are designed to withstand the harsh conditions of space travel. They are built to be lightweight, compact, and resistant to radiation and extreme temperatures. These systems allow for easy access and retrieval of media files while minimizing the risk of damage or data loss.

In addition to pre-recorded content, astronauts also have the option to stream live events or news broadcasts from Earth. This capability allows them to stay connected with current events and experience important moments in real-time while being thousands of miles away.

Watching TV shows on the moon not only provides entertainment for astronauts but also serves as a way to maintain a connection with life on Earth. It offers a sense of familiarity and normalcy in an otherwise extraordinary environment. Being able to relax and enjoy their favorite shows helps astronauts cope with the challenges and isolation that come with living in space for extended periods.

Furthermore, watching TV shows can also serve as a form of psychological support for astronauts. It provides them with an escape from the demanding nature of their work and allows them to decompress mentally. The ability to unwind through entertainment contributes to their overall well-being and helps maintain morale during long-duration missions.

Government Coverups

Government Covering Up Existence of Unicorns

Unicorns, mythical creatures with a single horn on their forehead, have captivated the human imagination for centuries. However, there is a growing belief among conspiracy theorists that the government is actively covering up the existence of unicorns. While this may seem far-fetched, it is important to explore the reasons behind such claims and consider whether there could be any truth to them.

One possible reason for the government's alleged cover-up is their desire to maintain control over society. Unicorns are often associated with magic and enchantment, and their existence could challenge established religious beliefs or scientific explanations. By suppressing information about unicorns, the government can ensure that people remain focused on more tangible matters and do not question the status quo.

Another motive for hiding the existence of unicorns could be related to national security. If unicorns possess extraordinary abilities or possess unique genetic traits, they could potentially be exploited by other countries or organizations for military purposes or economic gain. The government may fear that revealing the existence of these creatures would lead to a global race to capture and harness their powers.

Furthermore, it is worth considering whether the government's cover-up extends beyond mere secrecy and involves active manipulation of information. Conspiracy theorists argue that sightings of unicorns are deliberately dismissed as hoaxes or misidentifications in order to discredit those who claim to have encountered these mythical beings. This strategy serves to maintain public skepticism and prevent widespread belief in their existence.

Signs That the Government Is Lying

In a world where information is readily available at our fingertips, it can be challenging to discern fact from fiction. Conspiracy theories abound, and one common belief is that governments frequently lie to their citizens. While it is important not to fall into a trap of unfounded paranoia, there are indeed signs that can indicate when
the government may be hiding or distorting the truth.

One telltale sign that the government may be lying is inconsistency in their statements or actions. When officials provide contradictory information or change their stance on an issue without a reasonable explanation, it raises suspicions about their honesty and integrity. This inconsistency can manifest in various forms, such as conflicting statements from different government agencies or discrepancies between official reports and eyewitness testimonies. A good example would be mistaking a weather balloon for a flying saucer.

Another red flag is when governments resort to secrecy and withhold information without valid justifications. While certain matters may genuinely require confidentiality for national security reasons, excessive secrecy can create an atmosphere of mistrust and suspicion among citizens.

When governments consistently refuse to disclose information or invoke national security as a blanket excuse, it becomes difficult to determine whether they are genuinely protecting the public or hiding their own misdeeds.

A lack of transparency and accountability is another sign that the government may be lying. When officials evade questions, avoid public scrutiny, or dismiss legitimate concerns without providing satisfactory explanations, it erodes trust in their intentions. A government that is truly committed to serving its citizens should be open to dialogue, willing to address criticisms, and transparent about its decision making processes.

Hiding Pens in Area 51

Area 51, a highly classified United States Air Force facility located in the Nevada desert, has long been shrouded in secrecy and surrounded by conspiracy theories. Among the many speculations surrounding this mysterious base is the claim that the government is hiding pens within its confines. While this may seem trivial compared to other alleged cover-ups, it is worth exploring why such a theory exists and what it reveals about public perceptions of government secrecy.

The idea that pens are being hidden in Area 51 stems from a broader belief that the government possesses advanced technologies or knowledge that it refuses to share with the public. Conspiracy theorists argue that these pens could be prototypes of revolutionary writing instruments capable of defying gravity or even manipulating time and space. By keeping such groundbreaking inventions hidden, the government maintains its technological superiority while denying society access to potentially life changing advancements.

Another interpretation of this theory suggests that the pens symbolize something more significant than mere writing instruments. They represent a metaphorical tool used by the government to control information flow and manipulate public perception.

By hiding pens within Area 51, conspiracy theorists argue that the government seeks to suppress creativity, critical thinking, and free expression amongits citizens.

Furthermore, some proponents of this theory believe that hiding pens in Area 51 serves as a distraction from more significant secrets held within the base. By focusing on something seemingly inconsequential like pens, attention is diverted away from potentially more substantial cover-ups involving extraterrestrial technology or secret military experiments. This tactic allows the government to maintain control over the narrative and prevent deeper investigations into its activities.

Abducted Conspiracy Theorists by Aliens

Conspiracy theorists have long been fascinated by the idea of extraterrestrial life and their potential interactions with humans. While many conspiracy theories surrounding aliens focus on government cover-ups and secret agendas, there is a lesser-known theory that suggests that some conspiracy theorists themselves have been abducted by aliens.

According to this theory, certain individuals who are deeply involved in researching and uncovering government secrets become targets for alien abduction. These conspiracy theorists believe that their relentless pursuit of the truth has caught the attention of extraterrestrial beings who see them as a threat to their own hidden agendas.

One possible explanation for this phenomenon is that these conspiracy theorists possess knowledge or evidence that could potentially expose the existence of aliens or their collaboration with governments. By abducting these individuals, aliens may be attempting to silence them or erase any trace of their findings.

Government Coverup about Flying Chickens

Conspiracy theories often involve government cover-ups, but one particularly bizarre theory suggests that
governments are hiding the fact that chickens can fly. While it may sound absurd at first glance, this theory
raises interesting questions about what governments choose to disclose and why.

According to proponents of this theory, chickens
possess a natural ability to fly but have been genetically modified or selectively bred by governments to be flightless.

The reasoning behind this alleged cover-up varies from theory to theory. Some suggest that governments want to control the chicken population for agricultural purposes, while others propose more sinister motives such as using chickens as surveillance tools or even creating a secret army of flying chickens.

While there is no scientific evidence to support these claims, conspiracy theorists argue that there are historical accounts and folklore that suggest chickens were once capable of flight. They point to ancient artwork depicting flying chickens and stories passed down through generations as proof that something has changed over time.

One possible explanation for this phenomenon is that domestication and selective breeding practices have led to changes in chicken anatomy over centuries. Modern day domesticated chickens have been bred for specific traits such as meat production or egg-laying abilities, which may have inadvertently resulted in reduced flight capabilities.

Skeptics argue that the inability of modern chickens to fly is simply a result of natural selection and adaptation to their environment. They point out that chickens are heavy birds with relatively small wings, making sustained flight difficult for them.
While the idea of flying chickens may seem farfetched, it serves as a reminder that governments have the power to control information and shape public perception.

www.ingramcontent.com/pod-product-compliance
Lightning Source LLC
Chambersburg PA
CBHW070945080526
44587CB00015B/2231